W9-AZM-157

A Note to Parents

Dorling Kindersley Readers is a compelling new program for beginning readers, designed in conjunction with leading literacy experts, including Dr. Linda Gambrell, President of the National Reading Conference and past board member of the International Reading Association.

Beautiful illustrations and superb full-color photographs combine with engaging, easy-to-read stories to offer a fresh approach to each subject in the series. Each *Dorling Kindersley Reader* is guaranteed to capture a child's interest while developing his or her reading skills, general knowledge, and love of reading.

The four levels of *Dorling Kindersley Readers* are aimed at different reading abilities, enabling you to choose the books that are exactly right for your child:

Level 1 – Beginning to read
Level 2 – Beginning to read alone
Level 3 – Reading alone
Level 4 – Proficient readers

The "normal" age at which a child begins to read can be anywhere from three to eight years old, so these levels are intended only as a general guideline.

No matter which level you select, you can be sure that you are helping your child learn to read, then read to learn!

Dorling **DK** Kindersley

LONDON, NEW YORK, SYDNEY, DELHI, PARIS,
MUNICH and JOHANNESBURG

Designed and edited by Bookwork

For Dorling Kindersley
Managing Editor Bridget Gibbs
Senior Art Editor Sarah Ponder
Senior DTP Designer Bridget Roseberry
US Editor Reg Kahney
Production Shivani Pandey
Picture Researcher Frances Vargo
Jacket Designer Yumiko Tahata
Illustrator Peter Dennis
Indexer Lynn Bresler
Consultant Air Commodore Colin Foale
(father of Michael Foale)

Reading Consultant
Linda Gambrell, Ph.D.

First American Edition, 2000
2 4 6 8 10 9 7 5 3 1
Published in the United States by DK Publishing, Inc.
95 Madison Avenue, New York, New York 10016
Copyright © 2000 Dorling Kindersley Limited, London

Published in Great Britain by Dorling Kindersley Limited.

Library of Congress Cataloging-in-Publication Data

Royston, Angela
    Space station : accident on Mir / by Angela Royston.
    p. cm. -- (Dorling Kindersley readers)
    ISBN 0-7894-6685-6 (hc) -- ISBN 0-789406686-4 (pbk.)
    1. Space vehicle accidents--Juvenile literature. 2. Mir (Space
station)--Juvenile literature. [1. Mir (Space station) 2. Space vehicle
accidents] I. Title. II. Series.
    TL867 .R69 2000
    363.12'492--dc21
                                                    00-028023

Color reproduction by Colourscan, Singapore
Printed and bound in China by L Rex

The publisher thanks the following for their kind permission
to reproduce their photographs:
c=centre; t=top; b=below; l=left; r=right

Corbis: 9t (background), 11b, 39r; Reuters Newmedia Inc. 40l;
Ted Streshinsky 42bl; **Corbis Sygma**: Jacques Tiziou 9b, R.P.G. 21b;
Eurospace Centre, Transinne, Belgium: 27t; **John Frost Newspapers**:
'The Independent'/photo: AFP 16b; **Genesis**: 6-7, 12-13, 41b, 44t;
NASA: 3, 4t, 7t, 9tl, 10t, 15t, 17, 20t, 22tl, 25t, b, 32, 33r, 35b, 36t, 42t,
45, 46b, 47t, b, 49; **Novosti, London**: 14tl; **Popperfoto/Reuters**: 13r, 16t;
Viktor Korotayev 26l; NASA 36b; NASA/George Shelton 42-3; RTV 34;
Rex Features: Brendan Beirne 31b; **Science Photo Library/NASA**: 2, 8t,
10bl, 19t, 20b, 28tl, 29, 41t, 44b; **Frank Spooner Pictures**: Gamma/Laski
Diffusion 27b; **Topham Picturepoint**: 20br, 46; Associated Press 10br

Additional photography: Max Alexander 6t; Steve Gorton 4b, 12l,
15b, 35t; Alan Hills 19b; Gary Kevin 28b; Stephen Oliver 21t;
Susanna Price 22bl; Science Museum/James Stevenson 14bl

see our complete catalogue at
www.dk.com

Contents

SPACE STATION

ACCIDENT ON MIR

Written by Angela Royston

A Dorling Kindersley Book

Mike Foale
Michael Foale was born in Britain, but his mother is American. He moved to the U.S. because he wanted to become an astronaut.

NASA
These letters stand for National Aeronautics and Space Administration.

A great adventure

Jenna Foale gazed into the black nothingness of the night sky at Cape Canaveral, Florida. Her heart was thudding with excitement and fear. It was May 1997 and her father was about to be launched into space. A space shuttle would take him to Mir, the Russian space station that was circling around the Earth.

Jenna was five years old and her brother, Ian, was two. They did not know how dangerous the mission was, but they knew that they would miss their father while he was away.

Mike Foale was an astronaut. Like most American astronauts, he had spent only one or two weeks at a time in space before. This time, he was to live on the space station for four months. While he was there, he would be carrying out scientific experiments for the space organization NASA.

Mike Foale's mission would not be easy, but he had been preparing for it for a long time. He had trained with the Russian crew for 18 months and had learned to speak their language. At last the countdown to the launch had begun.

Growing seeds
One of Mike's experiments was to grow plants from seeds produced in space. The results would help future space station crews to grow their own food

High-rise
The fuel tank
of the space
shuttle is as
high as a five-
story building.
It carries
516,000 gallons
of fuel – as
much as ten
jumbo jets.

The space shuttle stood ready
on the launch pad. The spacecraft
Atlantis was perched high above the
ground, fixed to the back of a huge
fuel tank. Two rockets were also
fixed to the fuel tank. They would
boost the spacecraft into the sky
away from Earth.

Mike and the crew boarded
Atlantis just after midnight on
May 16, and at 2:30 a.m. the hatch
to the outside world was closed.
Jenna and her family watched
the launch pad from a
safe distance.

The launch pad was brightly lit, but just after 4:00 a.m. the lights around *Atlantis* went out. Jenna gripped her mother's hand. The countdown continued: "Five, four, three, two, one ..."

A blazing flame burst from below the space shuttle as the engines roared into action.

"... Lift-off of the space shuttle *Atlantis*."

Countdown
The launch was controlled by a team of people and computers. Someone relayed the countdown through a loudspeaker to the people watching.

Recovery
The rocket boosters drift down on parachutes and are recovered from the sea by ships. They are then used again on another shuttle mission.

Atlantis lifted off into the night amid the roar of the engines. Mike watched the launch tower slip past and felt the juddering of the rocket boosters. There was no going back now! Two minutes later, the rockets had burned all their fuel and fell away from the shuttle. Then the juddering stopped.

Fuel tank falls away

Spacecraft goes into orbit

Rocket boosters fall away

The watchers below saw the fiery trails of the falling rockets. For seven more minutes, the main engines took *Atlantis* higher and higher, until they had used up all the fuel in the tank. Then the huge empty tank also fell away, leaving the spacecraft to continue its journey on its own.

To everyone at Cape Canaveral, *Atlantis* was now just a speck of light in the night sky. The lift-off was completed! They all breathed a sigh of relief – except Jenna. "Daddy is turning into a star!" she sobbed. And indeed *Atlantis*, 200 miles above Earth, looked like a star in the sky.

Burnout
The fuel tank burns up as it falls through the air.

Space sounds
Space is silent, but it is not quiet inside the shuttle. Air has to be pumped around, and this makes lots of noise.

Space record
In May 1997, 10 astronauts, including Mike Foale, set a record for the number of people in one orbiting craft.

Mike and the crew were relieved and delighted to be safely in space. The engines were turned off and the only noise was the hum of the spacecraft's computers and machines. *Atlantis* began to circle Earth once every 90 minutes.

The view was amazing. First the astronauts saw continents, oceans, and clouds all bathed in beautiful, warm sunlight. Then, when the spacecraft traveled over the dark, night side of Earth, the astronauts could see the stars – many more than they could see from Earth, and much brighter.

A satellite image of Earth showing the dark and light side, or day and night

A view of the city of Tokyo, Japan, as seen from Atlantis.

Now the astronauts were weightless. This was because they were traveling so high and so fast around Earth that they could not feel the pull of gravity – the force that pulls everything toward the ground. When they undid their safety straps they floated about in the spacecraft.

The Grand Canyon in Arizona, as seen from Atlantis.

Hazards
In space, if you let go of something, it floats around. Everything has to be put away or strapped down carefully.

The crew began to prepare for the docking with Mir. The pilot slowly guided *Atlantis* closer and closer to Mir, until the two spacecraft were lined up exactly. Carefully, he slid *Atlantis* into one of Mir's docking hatches. The hatch doors between Mir and *Atlantis* opened and Mike was greeted by the two Russian cosmonauts on Mir, Sasha and Vasily.

The mission and space station were controlled by Ground Control – a team of computers, scientists, and experts in Russia. But Ground Control could communicate with Mir only when it was overhead.

Atlantis *docked with the Mir space station*

As soon as he could, Mike joined the Russian crew. He took off his NASA clothes and put on Russian cosmonaut clothes. The two crews unloaded supplies of water and equipment from *Atlantis*.

A few days later, *Atlantis* left Mir to return to Earth. Mike watched as it disappeared. It would be a long time before he saw his friends from NASA again.

Vasily Tsibliev
Vasily was the commander on Mir when Mike arrived.

Sasha Lazutkin
Sasha was an engineer. It was his first stay on Mir.

Repairs
Before Mike arrived, Mir's crew had been trying to find a leak in the cooling system.

Spektr

Node

The base block, where the Russians ate, washed, and slept

Kvant 2

13

Bit by bit
Mir was built
in space. Each
module was
attached one
by one. This is
Mir in 1986.

Space food
Space meals are
pre-prepared on
Earth, and the
food is put in
packs on a tray.
The astronauts
use fingers or
cutlery to eat
from one pack
at a time.

The Mir space station was made up of several modules. Mike floated from one to another using his hands and feet to push himself along the walls. The largest module was the living area where the Russians ate, washed, and slept. At one end was a round Node with hatches to other modules. One of these, Spektr, was where Mike slept.

Mike set up his experiments in the modules around the Node. These modules were already cluttered with machines and equipment. The module Kvant 2, for example, held the machines that made life in space possible. These included a machine called Elektron. It used waste water to make oxygen.

Sasha Lazutkin taking a photo inside Mir

All the machines used electricity. Solar panels on the outside of the station collected energy from sunlight and turned it into electricity. Machines called gyrodynes kept the station angled so that, as it turned, the solar panels always faced the Sun and the panels collected as much energy as possible.

Sun power
The electricity made in solar panels is stored in batteries. In space, it is used to provide heat and light and to power equipment.

15

Progress
The docking test for Progress was dangerous. Vasily had to maneuver the craft manually from 4 miles away from Mir to 160 ft away.

Bad news
On Earth, news of the crash on Mir soon appeared in newspapers and on television.

Disaster strikes

Things went well on Mir until June 25. Then disaster struck. Vasily was practicing a new way of docking the Progress supply ship. This craft brought new supplies from Russia and took away garbage. It had no crew so Vasily was operating it by remote control.

Suddenly, Vasily realized that the supply ship was coming toward them too fast. He tried to make it brake, but it was too late. Progress smashed into the solar panels on Spektr and then hit the module itself.

Mike heard a thud and then a hiss. Air was escaping from the space station. The crew was in great danger. If all the air escaped, they would die in minutes. The air pressure alarms began to ring. They were so loud that the men could not hear each other speak.

Sasha thought that Progress had made a hole in Spektr. He tried to shut the hatch so air would not escape from the whole station. But electricity cables were in the way.

Essential cables
Cables carried electricity from Spektr's solar panels to the rest of the space station.

Mir orbiting Earth after the accident

Damage to solar panels caused by Progress

Quickly, Mike came to help Sasha. They cut some of the cables and pulled out the plugs on the others. Then they slammed the hatch shut. They had stopped air escaping from the rest of the station, but they were not safe yet. Mir was spinning and tumbling in space, the solar panels had stopped making electricity, and the batteries were dangerously low.

Mike and Sasha switched off most of the batteries to save electricity. The lights went out and the space station became freezing cold. Then Mir moved into sunlight. The men could see again, but the station became boiling hot.

The situation was desperate but the cosmonauts had been trained to cope with emergencies. Elektron was not working, so they lit special candles that made oxygen instead of burning it so that they could breathe.

Freezing cold
On the dark side of Earth, the temperature in space is colder than the Antarctic.

Boiling hot
When the Sun shone on Mir, the temperature quickly rose and became hotter than the hottest desert on Earth.

Space disasters
Space travel is dangerous. In 1969 there was an explosion on *Apollo 13* that put the engine out of action. Mission Control worked out how to get the spacecraft home safely.

Quick getaway
A Soyuz spacecraft was always docked on Mir for the crew to use if they had to escape in an emergency.

The people at Ground Control tried to help the cosmonauts. The most important task was to stop the station from spinning. "What is your angle and speed?" they asked Vasily.

There was no instrument on board that could give the answer. Then Mike put his thumb to the window and estimated how fast it was moving compared to the stars. Now Ground Control was able to use Mir's engines to stop the space station spinning.

But the solar panels still did not face the Sun. Ground Control told Vasily to turn the space station by firing bursts of the thrusters in the docked spacecraft Soyuz – the craft that had brought Vasily and Sasha to Mir.

Mike again used the stars and the Sun to work out how long they should fire the thrusters. Easier said than done! The calculations were difficult and he was exhausted.

Vasily worked the engines. Mike wanted him to use more power but Vasily would not risk it. "We will need Soyuz to escape from Mir," he said. "If we use too much of its fuel, we will be stuck up here."

Ground Control discussing the problem on Mir

Star work
You can find out which way you are facing on Earth with a compass. It is much more difficult in space.

No toothbrush
When the hatch to Spektr was closed, Mike lost lots of his things including his sleeping bag, toothbrush, and clothes.

Sasha persuaded Vasily that Mike was right. It took 24 hours to turn Mir into the correct position, but at last the solar panels faced the Sun again and the batteries started recharging. Now the crew could get some sleep.

Although the living area had light, heat, and cooling again, there was not enough electricity to heat the other modules. Nearly half of Mir's electricity was made by the solar panels on Spektr, and the cables had been cut.

Ground Control had a plan. Vasily and Sasha would put on spacesuits, go into Spektr, and reconnect the cables. It would be like a spacewalk, or extravehicular activity (EVA) – a dangerous job. It was fixed for July 17.

Vasily and Sasha started to practice. Vasily thought that people blamed him for the accident and he wanted to put it right. But he was exhausted and anxious, and his heart was not beating properly. Ground Control thought that he might have a heart attack.

Cold comfort
Once Spektr was closed, Mike slept with his head in the Node and his feet in Priroda, an unheated module. Vasily lent him a sleeping bag because Mike's was in Spektr.

Spacewalk
The first person to do an EVA was cosmonaut Alexei Leonov. His spacewalk took place in March 1965.

Ground Control asked Mike if he would go with Sasha to reconnect the cables instead of Vasily. Mike was happy to do it, but NASA was worried. How safe was Mir now?

Mike and Sasha went on preparing for the "spacewalk." All the hatches into the Node had to be sealed shut to stop air from escaping when Mike and Sasha opened the hatch to Spektr. But more than 100 electricity cables passed through the Node. All of these cables had to be unplugged before the hatches could be sealed. The crew practiced unplugging the cables in the right order. This was important.

Two days before the "spacewalk," Sasha made a terrible mistake. He unplugged the cables that powered the gyrodynes, and Mir spun out of control again.

Once again Vasily and Mike had to use Soyuz's engines to turn Mir so that the solar panels faced the Sun. This time Vasily did exactly what Mike asked, and Mir was soon stable.

Working guest
Mike was a guest on Mir so he was not meant to help the Russians with their jobs. But after the accident he was able to help more and more.

Jumble
So many cables passed through Mir, that it was difficult to tell which cable was attached to which machine.

Help arrives

Two new Russian cosmonauts were due to go to Mir soon, and Ground Control decided that they should do the spacewalk. This meant that life on board the space station would be difficult for several more weeks.

On Earth, Anatoli Solovyev and Pavel Vinogradov practiced the spacewalk in a model of Spektr in a water tank – being underwater is the nearest thing on Earth to being weightless.

The cosmonauts launched into space on August 5 and arrived on Mir two days later. They took a new hatch for Spektr. It allowed cables to pass through it without letting air escape.

On August 14, after six months on Mir, Vasily and Sasha left in their Soyuz spacecraft to return to Earth. Mike was sad to say goodbye to them – they had survived so much together.

"I hope that everything bad leaves with us," said Vasily. He thought that while he had been on Mir he had brought bad luck to the space station.

Weightlessness
Astronauts can prepare for the weightlessness of space. The feeling can be simulated in a "five degrees of freedom chair."

Top right: "Five degrees of freedom chair" Eurospace centre, Transinne, Belgium

The new crew wasted no time. On August 16, Anatoli, Pavel, and Mike boarded the new Soyuz spacecraft, and Anatoli flew it around the outside of Mir so that they could see the damage.

Mike used a video camera to film the damage to Spektr. The film would be used to plan an EVA in which Anatoli and Mike could examine the damage more closely. This would take place after the spacewalk inside Spektr. They flew around Mir for 44 minutes before redocking.

The crew continued for many days to prepare for the internal spacewalk. Then bad luck struck again. Mir's main computer suddenly shut down. The space station began spinning and tumbling out of control again.

Anatoli and Pavel were alarmed, but Mike was used to it by now! "Don't worry," he said. "I've done this before!"

Mir on TV
Ground Control often set up a video link so that people on Earth could see Mir on TV.

Outside view of the damage to Mir

Out of time
The spacesuits had enough oxygen to last for only six hours.

Clean crystals
When Anatoli and Pavel entered Spektr, there were lots of tiny white crystals floating about. They were crystals from Mike's shampoo, which had separated because there was no air pressure to keep it together.

At last everything was ready for the internal spacewalk. On August 22 Anatoli and Pavel put on their spacesuits. The spacesuits provided oxygen for the men to breathe and protected them from the extreme heat and cold of space. Mike floated into Soyuz, where he waited during the spacewalk. If anything went badly wrong, they would all escape in Soyuz. Mike could talk to the other two by radio, but he could not see them.

The first spacesuits were made for only one particular astronaut, who wore it all the time. Now there are suits for different jobs, and they are reused.

Anatoli and Pavel sealed all the hatches to the Node. Then they removed all the air from the Node before opening the hatch to Spektr.

Using flashlights, Anatoli and Pavel looked around Spektr for the cables from the solar panels. Then they fitted the new hatch and began to reconnect the cables. It was hard work and it took them three hours. Before he left Spektr, Pavel gathered some of Mike's things, including a photo of his children.

Happy father
When Pavel told Mike he was bringing him the photo of his children, Mike said, "That will make me very happy."

It was one of the most difficult
repairs that had ever been made
in space. But the crew got their
reward. By the next day, the
batteries were fully charged and
all the modules had light and heat
again. Would the spacewalk outside
Mir also go well?

Ground Control had planned the
external spacewalk carefully. This
was the plan: Mike would be
tethered to Mir to stop him from
floating off into space. Anatoli
would be tethered to the end of a
long boom. Mike would hold the
boom while Anatoli tried to find the
hole in Spektr. If he found it, he
would fix it. Then the crew would be
able to use the module again.

By September 6 they were ready.
Mike and Anatoli put on their
spacesuits and went into the airlock
at the end of the module Kvant 2.
This special hatch had two doors.

Before the cosmonauts opened the outer door, they shut and sealed the inner door. This stopped all the air from rushing out of the space station. Then they floated out into the vast nothingness of space. Only the tethers kept them safe.

Precious air
Oxygen is precious in space. Experiments have shown that growing plants in space could provide valuable supplies of fresh oxygen.

No sound
There is no air and no sound in space. Mike and Anatoli floated silently in the endless space.

Spacewalk
During their six-hour EVA, Mike and Anatoli orbited Earth nearly four times. It took about 92 minutes for Mir to make one complete orbit of the planet.

Mike and Anatoli moved slowly from Kvant 2 across Mir to Spektr. Mike held the boom tightly and swung Anatoli toward the damaged module. As the hours ticked by, they moved through sunlight and darkness, over and over again. Mike loved the stillness.

Anatoli began to look for the hole in Spektr. He used a knife to cut into the material that covered the module. Pieces of it flew in all directions. Mike watched anxiously. If anything tore Anatoli's spacesuit, he would die. Even a small tear would make the suit useless.

Anatoli tried for hours to find the hole, but he could not find it. He moved the solar panels, though, so that they would collect even more sunlight. He also photographed the damage to Spektr close up. Then the two men reentered the airlock.

Space glove
During their spacewalk, Mike and Anatoli wore special gloves that left their fingers cold and tingling. Mike described it as being like putting his hand in snow.

The damaged solar panels

Next in line
Dave Wolf was the astronaut who replaced Mike on board Mir. He was originally going to go to Mir early in 1998, but his mission was brought forward.

New computer
The Russians asked the Americans to take a new computer to Mir on the space shuttle. It was made and programed in Russia.

The crew expected life on Mir to return almost to normal, and Mike began to look forward to going home. The space shuttle was due to arrive on September 26 to pick him up and bring another astronaut to take his place.

Then, just two days after the spacewalk, Mir's main computer failed again. Mir spun out of control and the crew had to reposition it.

"Thank goodness it didn't happen during our spacewalk!" said Mike, but he was worried. NASA was wondering whether it was safe to send another American astronaut up to Mir. Mike's return home to Earth might be delayed.

To Mike's relief, *Atlantis* launched on time on September 25 and docked with Mir two days later. When the hatches between Mir and *Atlantis* were opened, the shuttle commander stepped forward, holding a new computer. Anatoli accepted it with a huge smile.

OK for now
Cosmonauts finally installed the new Mir computer on October 3. After that, the station's computer troubles were over – but only for a while.

Re-usable
The shuttle spacecraft are used up to 100 times. *Atlantis* took Mike up to Mir and brought him home again.

Delay
The wind at Cape Canaveral was so strong on the day planned for Mike's landing that the landing was delayed for a day, until October 6.

Homeward bound

The hand-over took six days. Then, on Thursday, October 3, Mike left Mir to travel in *Atlantis* back to Cape Canaveral. Down on Earth, his family was longing to see him again. Jenna and Ian drew a "welcome home" poster.

Atlantis orbited until the people at NASA's Mission Control said it was safe to land.

On Sunday, the crew got the go-ahead to land, and Mike's family went to Cape Canaveral to watch. The pilot slowed down the spacecraft and it began to drop toward Earth. The crew switched off their radios and strapped themselves into their seats for landing.

Atlantis dropped through the thin air high above Earth at about 16,000 mph. The craft had no engines so it glided down.

Gradually, the air became thicker and thicker. Friction between the air and the falling spacecraft slowed down *Atlantis* but also made the outside red-hot. A heat shield protected it from the heat and stopped it from burning up.

Radio silence
When the crew switched off their radios to land, Mission Control lost contact with them. It then could not tell what *Atlantis* was doing. This happens between about 53 and 33 miles above Earth.

Thin air
The further you go from Earth, the thinner the air gets, until it fades out. This photograph of Earth, taken from space, shows how narrow the band of air is.

The pilot steered *Atlantis* toward the landing site. Soon the spacecraft was gliding no faster than a fighter jet – about 420 mph.

At Cape Canaveral, everyone watched the sky anxiously. For many minutes after reentry into the atmosphere, the experts at Mission Control had lost contact with *Atlantis*, but this was normal. At last they heard a dull sonic boom.

Minutes later a tiny speck appeared in the deep blue sky – *Atlantis* was nearly home!

There were just 14 seconds to touchdown. The pilot lowered the wheels and the craft landed on the runway.

Atlantis was still speeding at 255 mph. A kind of parachute ejected and ballooned out behind the craft to slow it down. Everyone cheered and Jenna and Ian jumped up and down with excitement.

"Welcome home. Excellent job," said Mission Control as *Atlantis* came to a halt.

Drag chute
The parachute that ejects behind the spacecraft is called a drag chute. It acts as a brake by dragging through the air.

Sickness
Astronauts can feel sick when they are in space. Mike felt sick when he landed.

Work out
Weightlessness in space can weaken muscles because moving around takes less effort. Astronauts must exercise for two hours a day to keep fit.

JFK
In 1960, U.S. President John F. Kennedy encouraged astronauts to go to the Moon. The Kennedy Space Center in the U.S. is named after him.

The astronauts waited for about an hour for the shuttle to cool down. Then they came out. Mike found it difficult to walk. Although he had exercised on Mir, his muscles had become weak. While he was weightless in space, he had not had to work as hard as he did on Earth. But nothing stopped him from hugging and kissing his family. "It's great to be back," he said, and Jenna and Ian agreed.

Mike spent that night with his family in rooms in the Kennedy Space Center.

He was asked what he would like to eat for his first meal back on Earth. "Lasagne and pizza, plus a lot of beer and chocolate," he replied.

Later, Mike said that being on Mir was the most difficult thing he had ever done, but he also remembered what President John F. Kennedy had once said: "We do not attempt things because they are easy, but because they are hard, and in that way we achieve greatness."

New strength
It took several weeks for Mike's muscles to get strong again.

Next mission
Crews were chosen for a space shuttle mission to Mir about two years in advance. This was the crew picked to fly in September 1997, including Mike Foale, who flew home with the crew.

Goodbye, Mir
Mir was left unmanned in 1999. In 2000, a Russian crew went up to see if Mir could be put back in use.

The story continues

Mir did not break down because it was badly built. In fact, it survived the crash with Progress only because it had been so well designed.

Both the Russians and the Americans wanted to keep Mir going. NASA paid for their astronauts to live on Mir to learn what it was like to spend a long time in space. Russia needed the money to fund their own space program. The astronauts wanted Mir to keep going too. A new space station was being planned and they wanted to get as much experience of long missions as possible.

The year after Michael Foale returned from Mir, American space shuttles and Russian rockets began to take the parts of the new space station into space.

The new space station is being launched into orbit around Earth, piece by piece. Europe, Japan, and Canada are helping to build it. This artist's impression shows what it will look like when it is completed.

Good advice
Mike was able to use his experiences on Mir to advise the people who are building the new space station.

Solar panels

Modules for laboratories and living quarters

Zarya control module was the first section to be put into orbit

Mike Foale hovers above Discovery's *cargo bay during a spacewalk to repair the Hubble Space Telescope.*

Space probes
Robotic space probes have visited all the planets in the solar system, except Pluto.

While the new space station is being built, spacecraft have continued to explore space. In 1997, an unmanned spacecraft landed on Mars, 35 million miles from Earth. A spacecraft was also launched that will reach Saturn in 2004.

In December 1999, Mike Foale went up in the space shuttle *Discovery*, this time to repair the Hubble telescope. This huge telescope is in orbit 380 miles above Earth. It takes clear pictures of

distant stars and galaxies. By 1999 it had been in space for nearly 10 years. Parts of it were wearing out and had to be replaced. The astronauts made three spacewalks on this mission in order to make the repairs.

Long journey
It took more than six months for the spacecraft carrying the Viking lander to reach Mars. Viking found no signs of life on the planet.

There will be many more space adventures. NASA may send astronauts to Mars, and there are plans to build a space station on the Moon. One day there may even be a hotel orbiting Earth. Who knows?

Gyroscopes
Astronauts Steven Smith and John Grunsfeld made repairs to the gyroscopes that kept Hubble pointing in the right direction.

Glossary

Air pressure
The force of air. The more air the greater the air pressure.

Airlock
A hatch with two doors from which air can be sucked out and pumped in.

Astronaut
A U.S. man or woman who travels into space.

Atlantis
The U.S. spacecraft that carried Michael Foale to and from Mir.

Battery
A device used to store electricity.

Boom
A long movable metal arm, like a fishing rod.

Charged
A battery is said to be charged when it is full of electricity.

Cosmonaut
The Russian word for an astronaut.

Countdown
A counted check down to zero, when a certain event, such as the lift-off of the shuttle, is planned to take place.

Docking
When two spacecraft, such as *Atlantis* and Mir, lock together in space.

EVA
Extravehicular activity, also called a spacewalk, when astronauts work outside their spacecraft in space.

Gravity
The force that pulls things toward Earth and gives them their weight.

Ground Control
The scientists and computers on Earth that control a space mission.

Hatch
A type of door. In space, hatches can be made airtight.

Heat shield
Tiles on a spacecraft that protect it from burning up as it falls through the air.

Mir
The space station in which Michael Foale lived for four months.

Module
A section of a space station or spacecraft.

Node
A module on Mir to which four other modules were joined, and where Soyuz was docked.

Oxygen
A chemical in the air that all living things need to breathe to stay alive.

Progress
An unmanned Russian spacecraft that brought supplies to Mir and took away garbage.

Remote control
Controlling something by computer from a distance.

Rocket boosters
Rocket engines that give the space shuttle power to launch into space.

Solar panel
A device that changes the energy in sunlight into electricity.

Soyuz
The name of Russian spacecraft that took cosmonauts to and from Mir and acted as emergency escape craft.

Space shuttle
U.S. spacecraft that are launched from Earth by rocket and return like gliders to land on a runway. They can be used again and again.

Spacesuit
Protective clothing worn by astronauts. Spacesuits that provide air, water, and warmth are worn during EVAs.

Spektr
The module on Mir that was hit in the collision with a Progress spacecraft.

LAKE COUNTY PUBLIC LIBRARY
INDIANA

Some materials may be renewable by phone or in person if there are
no reserves or fines due.   www.lakeco.lib.in.us   LCP#0390